Prosperity with a Purpose

Christians and the Ethics of Affluence

Prosperity with a Purpose

Christians and the Ethics of Affluence

Churches Together in Britain and Ireland
Bastille Court
2 Paris Garden
London SE1 8ND

info@ctbi.org.uk
www.ctbi.org.uk

Prosperity with a Purpose forum address: www.ctbi.org.uk/pwap

ISBN 0 85169 310 5

Published 2005 by CTBI

A catalogue record of this book is available from the British Library

Printed by Bercker in Germany

Cover design: Nial Smith Design

Contents

Foreword

The Churches are rightly concerned about poverty and put tremendous effort into working for its eradication. They have given less attention to prosperity. Yet, we in Britain and Ireland are living in an age of unprecedented increasing wealth, when questions about how prosperity should be understood and used are of the utmost importance.

That was why, in November 2001, the Church Representatives' Meeting – a regular meeting of senior representatives of the British and Irish Churches – commissioned a working group to undertake a study of prosperity. They were to take seriously the context of globalization, the persistence of terrible worldwide poverty, and the impact that our new riches have on the environment. They were to encourage widespread participation in their conversation, drawing on the different experiences of the different parts of these islands. They were to listen to differing viewpoints and perceptions. And they were to report in time to contribute to the debate ahead of the next UK General Election.

The group has fulfilled its task admirably. Two publications result. This slim volume, drafted by Clifford Longley, contains the study's conclusions and recommendations. The second, a fuller examination of the issues, is written by a number of authors and takes the form of a collection of essays. The first publication – *Prosperity with a Purpose: Christians and the Ethics of Affluence* – is the product of the CTBI working group, and as such is commended by the Church Representatives' Meeting of CTBI as a useful and important ecumenical contribution to the debate on prosperity. *Prosperity with a Purpose: Exploring the Ethics of Affluence* is the fuller companion volume containing essays arising from the group's reflection. It simply expresses the individual opinions of the authors themselves, carrying no authority other than that, but is designed as a volume in the hope of stirring up vigorous debate on the issues raised by each essay.

Particular thanks are owed: to Clifford Longley, for putting his writing skills at the group's disposal; to the members of the working group and all who fed ideas into its thinking; and lastly to John Kennedy, Coordinating Secretary for Church and Society for Churches Together in Britain and Ireland (CTBI), who has seen the project through from inception to completion.

I am delighted to add my own commendation. CTBI exists to promote cooperation and mutual learning between the Churches and nations of these islands, as they struggle to engage meaningfully with contemporary society. It seeks to do this in a way that witnesses to Christian unity, and beyond that to the unity of all humankind. This report is a good example of that process in action, and what it says deserves to be heard.

David Goodbourn
General Secretary
Churches Together in Britain and Ireland

Introduction

The Christian social conscience in Britain and Ireland has no single organized voice, but *Prosperity with a Purpose: Christians and the Ethics of Affluence* comes closer to that voice than anything previously published. It has only been made possible because the thinking of all the mainstream denominations on the socio-economic issues of the day has converged around one key proposition: that under the right conditions, economic growth can serve God's purposes.

These conditions are:

- That humanity is seen as one human family, with a universal bond of solidarity;

- That wealth creation and the pursuit of social justice are inextricably linked;

- That market forces encourage economic growth but are regulated in the interests of the community;

- That the environment is safeguarded by substantial efforts to mitigate the harm caused by pollution;

- That advancing prosperity leaves no-one behind; not children, retired people, those who care for families, disabled people, nor any other section that is vulnerable or liable to neglect;

- That globally, priority is given to those whose economies are burdened by unmanageable international debt, or those who are victims of unfair international trading conditions;

- That the structures of civil society are renewed so that local communities can shape their own future.

Measured by these conditions, progress is patchy. Poverty is reducing in some sections, increasing in others. Economic growth and the current Government's 'welfare to work' policy have demonstrated that there is enough work for everyone and that work is an effective route out of poverty. But in many regions the policy is stalling, reaching the limit of what it can achieve. Large pockets of poverty stubbornly persist. New policies will be necessary, including a review of the reliance on means testing which is producing serious injustices and anomalies.

The two previous studies influencing *Prosperity with a Purpose* set a new pattern for Christian participation in public life. *The Common Good,* published by the Catholic Bishops of England and Wales in 1996, established the fundamental principle that market forces should be society's servants, not its masters. *Unemployment and the Future of Work*, published by the Council of Churches for Britain and Ireland in 1997 (the body preceding Churches Together in Britain and Ireland), exploded the myth that unemployment, and the human cost going with it, were inevitable.

Both studies recognized the vitality of market economies and their crucial role in wealth creation. This new study takes the debate a stage further: exploring the conditions under which true prosperity can be achieved and how it is to be defined. The challenge is not confined to politicians; all citizens have a role to play in creating a more just and sustainable society.

Principles and Proposals

- No policy which disadvantages the poor in order to benefit any other more privileged sector can expect a Christian blessing. (page 14)

- Those who engage in economic enterprise also have obligations to the common good. They deserve proper recognition when they seek to discharge their moral and social responsibilities. (16)

- The Christian ethic has to ask: what sort of people do we need to be, in order to bring about this state of prosperity and to share its fruits justly? This shifts attention from economic considerations to moral ones. (20)

- Human freedom does not thrive on superabundance. Someone who 'has everything' is unlikely to value any of it, having genuinely chosen none of it. (22)

- Consumerism values only what can be consumed. Consumerism emphasizes passivity, thus isolating individuals from their communities. (23)

- Christian thinking concerning wealth has to take seriously the example of the 'rich young man' in the gospels ... But Jesus concluded his parable by saying 'with God all things are possible'. (23)

- The economy can be managed so as to impoverish some as well as to enrich others. It is the responsibility of those engaged in politics to reconcile the outcomes of the market economy to the demands of the common good. (24)

- A further threat to the productive functioning of a market economy comes from the attempt to squeeze too much out for socially desirable ends. (26)

- A prosperous society is not one where certain groups are excluded from participation through poverty. Intense public consultation and debate will be required to create a consensus about what a 'decent minimum' income might be. (27)

- Entrepreneurship is of great service to the common good, meets humanity's deep need to be inventive and creative, and deserves proper reward. (28)

- There is a reasonable case, in the interests of social justice, for a higher-still rate on those earning three or four times the average income, as there is also a reasonable case for removing those on half the median income from income tax altogether. (28)

- Too often directors or senior managers seem to receive what amounts to a reward for failure. Thus it is right for the Government to review company law to see to what extent shareholders could gain greater control over boardroom pay as well as other aspects of company policy. (29)

- Justice cannot be done in some of the hard choices facing a market economy society if the mass media ignore, trivialize, slant or unduly personalize their coverage of them. (30)

- The Churches are well used to playing their part in a vibrant civil society, and look to the renewal of civil society as an essential element in the service of the common good. (31)

- The minimum wage can be used as a way of ensuring that all forms of work available are worthwhile. (44)

- The 'right to a living wage' is a right that can be met jointly by an employer and by the state. (44)

- Those, particularly women, who shoulder responsibilities, must be protected from unfair discrimination in pay, promotion, conditions of work and pension arrangements, or any diminution in professional esteem. (45)

- Except as a short-term necessity, the employment culture which judges employees by their willingness to work excessive hours is harmful to personal and family life and therefore contrary to a Christian ethic of work. (46)

- The Government's anti-poverty strategy of encouraging paid work has built-in limits to its effectiveness, both in relieving poverty itself and in producing a fairer society. (48)

- An individual on benefits quickly discovers that earning extra money results in a corresponding tapering off of benefits or credits. This has an effect similar to a high marginal rate of taxation, manifestly undesirable. (48)

- A wider spread of policies is needed than the present focus on employment as the only effective answer to poverty. (48)

- Those who are most income-deprived are usually also deprived of credit and of capital, and those obstacles are equally marks of poverty. Rates of interest, especially to the poor, ought to be subject to a ceiling; credit unions should be encouraged. (48)

- It is unfair to tax those who manifestly do not have enough money to live on. (48)

- There is perplexed talk of the 'stubborn refusal' of poverty to respond to measures designed to relieve it. A complete review of the national anti-poverty strategy is now due, perhaps by an independent body of high standing such as a Minimum Income Standards Agency. (49)

- The argument of principle for restoring the connection with average income rather than the rate of inflation is that retired people should, as a matter of justice, be entitled to share automatically in the growth of national prosperity - and that they should not have to submit to a means test in order to do so. (50)

- The biggest players in the global economy (the United States and the European Union) have tended to regard globalization as an opportunity to increase their economic strength rather than to put it at the service of the global common good. (52)

- The moral case for contributing a greater share of national wealth to the relief of poverty overseas is a compelling one. (52)

- The development of international institutions to regulate international markets has lagged behind. This leaves some of the world's poorest and most vulnerable people open to great hardship and injustice. (53)

- Methods for the regulation of global capital flows, (sometimes critically damaging to weak national economies) need urgent investigation. (53)

- The pretence that there is no problem of global warming is grossly irresponsible and unethical. Economic conditions have to be reshaped in order to deal with this problem, and while much can be achieved by the Kyoto Agreement on emissions-trading, the problem calls for a far more radical and more equitable sharing of emission costs. (53)

- Nature has been generous so far in providing the conditions for life to exist. But science can offer no guarantee that that generosity will continue, and religion can only offer a warning that it may not. (54)

- The Christian Churches of these islands now regard it as one of their prime tasks to cultivate a religious sense of humility and awe towards the natural world; to replace the exploitative culture of previous generations that Christianity itself was mistakenly thought to sanction. (54)

PROSPERITY WITH A PURPOSE

THE ETHICS OF PROSPERITY

Because they believe in a transcendent reality, Christians can offer their neighbours a word of genuine hope amidst the uncertain flux of history. The very possibility of prosperity for the many and not just the few is a new factor in the history of human civilization, which will demand the fashioning of new forms of wisdom.

Any ethical reflection on prosperity has to begin with the inalienable dignity and infinite value of the individual human person, who, nevertheless, only thrives in community. Every man and woman has the right to prosper, but also the responsibility to recognize that others have the same right. A well-ordered community - local, national and global - will be one in which individual and social rights and responsibilities are in balance, serving the general common wealth.

Every man and woman has the right to prosper

Christians wish to contribute both to a description of that well-ordered society, and towards its achievement. One of their contributions will be to underline the new global reality - that while national governments are vital links in the chain of decision-making, humanity must from now on think globally. That is a shift of consciousness of vast significance.

Humanity must now think globally

A well-ordered global society will have to be one in which there is a united commitment to overcome poverty, to create and distribute wealth fairly and wisely, and to advance human progress and development. But human beings, who have so much to gain from such a project, can also stand in its way. As long-term economic growth transforms the planet for the better, it can unleash forces that undermine that transformation. Prosperity has its paradoxes. Because of their reading of human nature, Christians believe that those who expect to build a perfect society here on earth will be disappointed. It is precisely in the midst of such setbacks and disappointments that hope in God offers encouragement to go on.

A well ordered society will overcome poverty, create and distribute wealth fairly and advance human progress and development

No policy which disadvantages the poor... can expect a Christian blessing

The Government's present emphasis on work as the favoured route out of poverty seems to be meeting in-built limitations

Do people still suffer in prosperous societies? What are the hazards of affluence? Is prosperity enough? These concerns cannot be limited to the present age

The Christian Churches of these islands share a commitment to social justice, nationally and globally, which flows from a deep conviction that Christ himself commands them to identify and oppose injustice and oppression committed against any person, regardless of status or description. Increasingly acting together, they have accepted that it is their duty to stand alongside the marginalized and excluded. Though such individuals and groups are not usually nowadays classified as 'the poor', the biblical use of that term clearly encompasses a wider definition than plain destitution. This orientation by the Churches is therefore sometimes described as a 'preferential option for the poor', whose interests should always be considered ahead of all other claims. No policy which disadvantages the poor (understood in these terms) in order to benefit any other more privileged sector can expect a Christian blessing.

In the course of the preparation of this document, existing and alternative anti-poverty programmes have been examined and none of them have been found fully satisfactory. Numerous reports have been noted of a widespread 'stubborn refusal' of poverty to respond to policies designed to deal with it, and the policies are therefore seen to be in danger of stalling. In particular, the Government's present emphasis on work as the favoured route out of poverty seems to be meeting in-built limitations, suggesting that most of the benefits from it may have been achieved and that new strategies will be required for further progress.

The more prosperous a society becomes, the more important it is for social justice and community cohesion that nobody be left behind. Thankfully, in many nations poverty is in at least sporadic retreat, and the experience of prosperity is spreading in its place. Before there is any prospect of prosperity becoming universal, however, certain basic questions have to be addressed. How is prosperity achieved and what does it consist of? What are the obstacles in its way? How does one even know that it has arrived? Does the arrival of prosperity banish any need for a concept of social justice? Do people still suffer in prosperous societies? What are the hazards of affluence? Is prosperity enough?

These concerns cannot be limited to the present age. Threats to the well-being of future generations, for instance through the degradation of the global environment, are of equal priority to threats to this generation. Churches and politicians must together give prophetic voice to the rights of generations as yet unborn, against the clamorous demands of those now living.

Threats to future generations, through the degradation of the environment are of equal priority

Social justice is not merely about providing safeguards for the least fortunate or most disadvantaged. It is also about mutual responsibility at all levels, and a shared commitment to the common good. Such a commitment will not be fostered if economic conditions are seen to be unfair, especially in the way the fruits of economic prosperity are distributed, nor if the wealthier and more powerful sections of society are seen to opt out of responsibility for the welfare of the rest.

Many people who do not see themselves as poor are nevertheless anxious, bitter, lonely, tired and sad

NEW CHALLENGES TO JUSTICE

New conditions present new challenges to the Churches' understanding of social justice. Those who suffer actual material deprivation in the form of hunger or homelessness must take priority, but economic forces can create other less visible forms of hardship or injustice which are more difficult to unravel or address. The challenges to human happiness come in many forms, in the imbalance between work and personal life, in the breakdown of community, and in deterioration and insecurity in the physical and social environment. Many people who may not see themselves as poor are nevertheless anxious, bitter, lonely, tired and sad. There is a spiritual malaise and a different kind of poverty – and hence a different kind of social injustice – present themselves in all these conditions. Social justice is not exclusively a matter of economics.

Social justice is not exclusively a matter of economics

A purely negative appraisal of economic activity is unacceptable

A purely negative appraisal of economic activity is unacceptable and an injustice to those engaged in it. Economic activity is instead something to celebrate. When it raises the standard of living of the population while relieving the lot of the poor, it is part of God's will for humanity. There is a need to redress a perceived imbalance in the way Christians have regarded the creation of wealth by economic activity. They should recognize that it is one of the chief

Christians have to recognize that it is one of the chief engines of progress and greater well being and to thank God for it

The pursuit of profit as an end in itself frequently results in hardship and injustice

engines of progress and greater well-being in the modern age, both directly and indirectly; and thank God for it.

But the pursuit of profit as an end in itself does frequently result in hardship and injustice. A market-based economy, given free rein, can increase both wealth and poverty. Though this may be the result of the outworking of economic laws, such laws are not sovereign and market forces must stand under judgement. Where they detract from the common good, they will need to be restrained. So governments may legitimately intervene to correct injustices resulting from free-market enterprise, and not just those which result from the failure of market mechanisms themselves.

Those who engage in economic enterprise also have obligations to the common good. They deserve proper recognition when they seek to discharge their moral and social responsibilities, which include commitment to honest and equitable trading practices, and to fair remuneration for their present and past employees. But good business practice can never ignore the impact of economic enterprise on the wider community.

Engaging in commerce of any kind depends upon the existence of respect, trust and honesty

Most corporations in the private sector are eager to conduct themselves as good corporate citizens and to be seen to do so, both by the way they behave commercially and also by such means as sponsorship and charitable donations, as well as their direct support for non-commercial activity for the good of the community. They know that the very possibility of engaging in commerce of any kind depends upon the existence of at least a minimum level of respect, trust and honesty between participants in the economic process. It is a matter of concern to business people as much as it is to church people when society seems to be heading away from those minimum levels of trust and honesty. The generation of economic capital requires the presence in the community of a stock of moral capital. If business behaves without a moral compass, it depletes the moral capital in the community which is essential for the conduct of its own affairs. Sooner or later business itself would become impossible. The inclusion of business ethics as a systematic part of management training is a positive sign that this need

The generation of economic capital requires the presence of moral capital

is being recognized, but the message has not yet permeated the whole business community.

Christians cannot limit their concerns to geographical frontiers but must have an interest and involvement in global justice. They cannot wish their own countries to prosper at the expense of others less fortunate. That insistence requires them to adopt a model which they can promote internationally as well as nationally. They are aware of the hardships and injustices that can follow from unfair international trading conditions and from the gross anomalies of international finance, especially through the burden of debt owed by poorer countries to richer countries. They are also aware that globalization presents new challenges to national and international regulators, which they have not yet answered. Hence the Churches are increasingly willing to act internationally, alongside NGOs (especially those linked to member churches such as Christian Aid and Cafod), to monitor the conduct of global business and to campaign for remedies when it abuses its power.

Christians are aware of the burden of debt owed by poorer countries to richer

Globalization presents new challenges to national and international regulators

Some limitations in the enjoyment of prosperity today may have to be imposed if the prospect of prosperity tomorrow is not to be severely jeopardized. This may require a drastic reappraisal of the way Christianity has traditionally regarded the created world, and the learning of a new sense of religious respect for the whole of creation and everything in it. The refinement and propagation of a Christian spirituality suitable to these new forms of environmental awareness is urgent, though made easier by the instinctive feeling shared by many people that the relation of humanity to the living world requires humility, awe and reverence. These are readily understood as spiritual and religious values, though they may still need theological interpretation and formal liturgical expression in a Christian context.

The relation of humanity to the living world requires humility awe and reverence – spiritual and religious values

Christians have to be aware of the complexity and interdependence of the many factors involved. Moral principles applied simplistically and without due respect for economic analysis can easily lead to erroneous solutions. So the Churches need the input of those of their members who possess expertise in this field, as well as the work of specialists in social ethics from the various religious traditions, past and

Moral principles applied simplistically can easily lead to erroneous solutions

Ecumenical progress presents a powerful new synthesis of witness and teaching

present. Yet ecumenical progress presents the possibility of a powerful new synthesis of witness and teaching. Blended together into a coherent whole, these resources could constitute a distinctively contemporary Christian social ethic that might be the common property of all of them, and could thus become an offering from the Churches of Britain and Ireland to other Churches elsewhere, where there are similar concerns. It is equally an offering to the community at large, which is made ill at ease by the absence of a coherent unifying project of social justice.

This must necessarily be an incomplete and continuous process, and presupposes a wider dialogue between the Churches and the societies in which they exist. Therefore not all the conclusions reached by a study such as this will be acceptable to everyone, nor will they be beyond criticism and improvement. All the questions raised will have to be revisited, both in the light of responses to this study and as conditions change. While the key principles derived from Christian faith are broadly unchanging, their application in particular circumstances must always be open to review.

The community at large is made ill at ease by the absence of a coherent unifying project of social justice

Christians particularly want to contribute to the national debates that will precede the next General Election for the Parliament at Westminster, as well as elections to national parliaments and assemblies in Scotland, Wales and Northern Ireland. In order to assist them, representatives from the Churches have made themselves familiar with the political approaches of the three main parties represented at Westminster, and have had conversations with senior figures from those parties. Church representatives are eager to listen to responses to this document from the political parties, which they hope will become part of a continuous dialogue.

None of the Churches participating in this study wish to be seen to be telling their members how to vote. Nor are the considerations raised in this study the only ones that voters need to address. This document is designed to make a genuinely non-partisan contribution in a partisan climate.

Christian social ethics is a broad river with many tributaries

The Christian insights represented here are not peculiar to any particular denominational tradition, and Christian social ethics is a broad river with many tributaries. Some of the greatest progress towards social justice in the past was achieved by prophetic voices in the Evangelical and Free Church traditions, such as those of Wilberforce, Shaftesbury and Booth, while two of the key documents which have inspired the present study are *Unemployment and the Future of Work - An Enquiry for the Churches* published by the Council of Churches for Britain and Ireland (the body preceding CTBI, sponsor of the present study) in 1997; and *The Common Good and the Catholic Church's Social Teaching*, a statement by the Roman Catholic Bishops' Conference of England and Wales in 1996. Both were published prior to the May 1997 General Election. Subsequently the Irish Catholic Bishops' Conference produced a report, *Prosperity with a Purpose*, which examined the problems of a society with a growing modern economy; and the Salvation Army published reports by the Henley Centre, *The Paradox of Prosperity and The Responsibility Gap*. These publications stand alongside a wide variety of other inputs from which this study has benefited. These sources include the papers prepared specially for it, which appear in *Prosperity with a Purpose: Exploring the Ethics of Affluence*, published for the first time and simultaneously with this document (see page 61). Those papers only carry the authority of their authors; this document, by contrast, the product of wide collaboration and consultation, is commended as a contribution to discussion by the Church Representatives' Meeting of Churches Together in Britain and Ireland.

Prosperity with a Purpose: Christians and the Ethics of Affluence is commended as a contribution to discussion by the Church Representatives' Meeting of Churches Together in Britain and Ireland

Prosperity with a Purpose: Exploring the Ethics of Affluence carries only the authority of its authors

PROSPERITY, SELF-INTEREST AND THE COMMON GOOD

One of the primary aims of democratic government is the promotion of the good of the people: the common good. Over many generations in many societies, one of the major threats to the good of the people has been absolute poverty - the inability to obtain the necessities of life such as food and water, warmth and shelter, clothing and health care. Even those who enjoyed a standard of living above the minimum lived with the ever-present threat of dropping down if their fortunes changed. The threat of disease affected all classes, as did the dangers of falling victim to crime and social disorder. Education and access to leisure became necessities relatively late; later still came demands that people should

'Prosperity' – the absence of poverty?

19

Prosperity includes sufficiency of wealth, pleasure and happiness, civilisation and culture, and longevity including good health

Industrialization and urbanization were by no means universal blessings

A modern economy needs a disposition towards morality, or it will be a thieves' kitchen

be protected by social insurance from the worst misfortunes that could befall them.

Industrialization and urbanization were by no means universal blessings, and among parts of the population poverty and hardship increased. But gradually the wealth that industrialization created spread out into the population at large, partly as the result of deliberate policies of redistribution and partly because the lifting up of the whole did, sooner or later, benefit the parts.

In the process, an identifiable ingredient in the aspirations of the people came to be known by the name 'prosperity,' the promise of which became a constant in the political debates of the 20th century. It meant simply the absence of poverty, defined in raw terms, but it has gradually come to mean the progressive raising of living standards, if not consistently year on year, then at the very least, generation by generation.

The word 'prosperity' is still often used in that narrower sense. But it has taken on deeper meanings, not least as the acquisition of material blessings is increasingly seen to bring with it factors which reduce, rather than enhance, the enjoyment of them. Thus prosperity widened into a more general aim; the promotion of the good of the people. One way of defining this new and richer meaning of prosperity is as the very reverse of Thomas Hobbes' description of 'life in an unregulated state of nature' - as 'solitary, poor, nasty, brutish, and short.' So prosperity is the opposite of all of those, not just the second of them. It includes participation in community, sufficiency of wealth, pleasure and happiness, civilization and culture, and longevity including good health.

Christian ethics should stay in step with this evolution in understanding. One way to do so is by asking: what sort of people do we need to be, to bring about this state of prosperity and to share its fruits justly? That question shifts attention from economic considerations to moral ones. A complex modern mixed economy needs a certain disposition towards morality, otherwise all it will be is a thieves' kitchen heading for a prompt return to the unregulated state of nature described by Thomas Hobbes.

It is a mistake to assume that gross social injustice must always result from a severe degree of wrong-doing by bad people. Sometimes 'structures of sin' take on a life of their own. The concept of structural sin illuminates how small acts of selfishness, neglect or moral blindness by a relatively small number can sometimes be magnified, through the leverage of economic mechanisms, until great harm is done to large numbers. The concept helps both sides to see where responsibility lies for the problem and what may be done about it. The damage done to poor national economies by an unsustainable level of international debt is a good example.

Morality - virtue - needs to be pursued as an end in itself, and as necessary for the building up of the common good in all aspects. Equipping people for prosperity by education in virtue, however, is not the primary task of governments, though they may legitimately concern themselves with it. In a religiously plural society, every faith community will want its own input to that process and will want to emphasize the importance of a holistic approach that does not neglect the spiritual dimension. Parents have a fundamental role, and so do professional teachers. The tone of a culture, to a considerable degree set by the mass media, will also be significant in setting the moral climate. So will the legal system. To the extent that all these components encourage virtue and discourage vice, they are helping to enhance prosperity. In so far as they encourage vice, they are the enemy of prosperity. And it will therefore be seen that prosperity has many enemies in modern society, some of whom masquerade as its friends.

In the process the word moves towards the true sense contained in its own structure: 'prosperity' comes from 'to prosper,' meaning to flourish or thrive. These moral concepts have never referred exclusively to an economic state but to general good fortune or well-being. This raises the question of human potential, which is a profoundly religious question. What is the ideal, towards which all human development ought to be channelled? Christians may look for an answer in 'the imitation of Christ', but they will also want to say that that demands a commitment to the pursuit of individual

Morality needs to be pursued as an end in itself

Prosperity has many enemies in modern society – some masquerade as its friends

Sometimes 'structures of sin' take on a life of their own

The question of human potential is a profoundly religious question

and social justice. A justified person is also a just person, in theological terms.

Once basic necessities are taken care of, the desire for greater prosperity manifests itself in other ways, as new dimensions of human flourishing come into view. One of the most important and noble of these is human freedom, perceived not just as the ability to make consumer choices but to choose freely what is truly good. *Free will is basic to human nature, part of God's design.* Included in the freedom God has granted humanity is the freedom to make bad choices, because God's wisdom saw that any other sort of freedom would not be true freedom. *Without the freedom to choose badly, morality is stunted: the person coerced into goodness is not really virtuous at all.*

Virtue is the facility to make right choices, especially when wrong choices have their own attractions. But the liberty that God wants humanity to enjoy extends beyond the moral sphere, where conscience reigns, and includes selecting from many available options those which most express and enhance the unique individuality and character of the person. Thus the individual can become more nearly what they were meant to be, fulfilling God's purpose in creating them. They, in turn, 'create' their own lives; and that too is human creativity at work.

Prosperity, in this area, means not only having a rich variety of choices, the better to match each person's individuality, but also each individual having the means to make such choices. But choice, as a morally desirable exercise of the faculty of freedom, also involves self-denial. Human freedom does not thrive on superabundance. *Someone who 'has everything' is unlikely to value any of it, having genuinely chosen none of it.*

Herein lies one of the greatest contradictions of a society mainly geared to consumerism. A wide variety of goods enables purchasers to select the best, thus obliging those who produce the rest either to raise their standards or lower their prices, or risk going out of business. That is how competition drives up quality and value-for-money. But *consumerism is an all-consuming ideology.*

Free will is basic to human nature, part of God's design

Without the freedom to choose badly, morality is stunted: the person coerced into goodness is not really virtuous at all

Someone who has everything is unlikely to value any of it, having chosen none of it

Consumerism is an all consuming ideology

Personal interactions can easily seem synonymous with the consumption of goods, so all relationships are seen as a form of commercial transaction offering immediate mutual benefits. The reality is often different: the pursuit of 'best price' can seriously disadvantage producers and lead to the exploitation of workers forced to accept low wages and poor conditions. Consumers have an ethical responsibility to take into account the human costs as well as the market price of the goods they purchase.

Consumerism measures people by what they possess rather than by their talents and achievements

Consumerism values only what can be consumed. Consumerism emphasizes passivity, thus isolating individuals from their communities. Consumerism measures people by what they possess rather than by their talents and achievements. Those who are unable to afford what they consider their share of consumer goods are liable to feel resentment. While wealth brings the expansion of choice, it can also bring over-attachment to material goods and physical benefits; and the consumerism a market economy relies on can degrade moral, social and cultural values.

All who leave this life, rich or poor, have to pass through the eye of a needle

Christian thinking concerning wealth has to take seriously the example of the 'rich young man' in the gospels, who was too attached to his possessions to take up the offer of eternal life. He was prepared to serve God, but not if he could no longer serve Mammon too. All who leave this life, rich or poor, have to pass through the eye of a needle - through which they cannot take their bags and baggage. It is as well they cultivate that attitude of mind long before the time comes for them to leave this world, otherwise they will find their attachment to possessions has become so habitual they cannot free themselves from it. The eye of the needle will be too narrow for the camel. But Jesus concluded his parable by saying 'with God all things are possible'. In a framework of social justice, wealth creation is no longer the pursuit of Mammon, a rival to the true God, but a service to humanity and way out of poverty into true prospering.

Wealth creation can create economic conditions in which the total available wealth increases

Jesus' reply to the young man, in any event, makes it clear that his obsessive attachment to possessions was the enemy of his true freedom and therefore of his true happiness, in this life as well as the next. In any full sense, he did not prosper. As others have discovered, once a certain level of material success has been achieved, further affluence does not lead automatically to happiness, and often leads away from it.

POVERTY, PROSPERITY AND THE MARKET ECONOMY

A Christian ethic which paid insufficient attention to the economic dimension of prosperity would fall a long way short of adequate. Some of the routes to social justice are economic, as are some of the causes of social injustice. In this respect, therefore, the broader and narrower meanings of the word prosperity converge. This becomes particularly clear once economic development ceases to be seen as 'zero-sum' - that is to say, a situation where giving more to some necessarily means giving less to others. In such situations, social justice would largely be a matter of redistributing a finite and limited amount of wealth. But wealth creation within the market system is not subject to such zero-sum limitations. It can create economic conditions in which the total of available wealth increases, so more can be given to some, and yet more to others.

Wealth creation is not subject to zero-sum limitations

However this effect is not inevitable. The economy can be managed so as to impoverish some as well as to enrich others. It is the responsibility of those engaged in politics to reconcile the outcomes of the market economy to the demands of the common good. The key is the management of the relationship between the dynamic market economy, government, and citizen.

This obligation on those engaged in the political process is rarely stated explicitly. The following statement from the draft Constitutional Treaty of the European Union is an exception; if adopted, it will become a guiding principle of European and national economic and political management for generations to come. (Even if not formally adopted such principles will certainly continue to shape the way the EU operates for the foreseeable future. Nor is this particular passage part of the current controversy about the adoption of the Constitution.)

It is the responsibility of those engaged in politics to reconcile the outcomes of the market economy to the demands of the common good

The Union shall offer its citizens an area of freedom,

security and justice without internal frontiers, and a single market where competition is free and undistorted. The Union shall work for the sustainable development of Europe based on balanced economic growth, a highly competitive social market economy, aiming at full employment and social progress, and with a high level of protection and improvement of the quality of the environment.

This European model, when working properly, relies upon the initiative of innovators and entrepreneurs to create and sustain successful businesses. If they fail, it fails. They have a 'right of enterprise', which is part of the basic human right to engage in creative work. Directly or indirectly they employ, and thereby bring prosperity to, workers, managers, suppliers, distributors and retailers; and meet the needs of consumers. Taxation revenue is generated by this successful process, which in turn makes possible extensive levels of public expenditure. The various markets required by these complex cycles of business are regulated in the name of society to ensure fair competition, health and safety, environmental and consumer protection, access to employment without discrimination with a decent level of wages and pensions, and so on. Provided the levels of regulation and taxation are not such as to cripple economic growth, the result is a virtuous circle of wealth creation and public revenue on the one hand and public and private investment on the other. In this climate productivity increases, and workers acquire ever more valuable skills in return for higher pay. Such societies generate wealth which can be directed to such socially desirable ends as the relief of poverty, the treatment of illness, pensions for the retired and improvement of the general social fabric.

Possible threats to market economies include: a breakdown of regulation because of lack of will; political favouritism or corruption; particularly inadequate controls on cartels or monopolies; loss of respect for instruments of government which are not seen as serving the common good; loss of confidence in the political process through cynicism; misconduct of politicians; or excess centralization; and a breakdown in the flow of reliable information; necessary for the democratic and regulatory processes to be scrutinized and for markets to function effectively.

Entrepreneurs have a 'right of enterprise', part of the basic human right to engage in creative work

A virtuous circle of wealth creation and public revenue and public and private investment

Threats to the productive functioning of a market economy

In addition, services traditionally provided by the public sector are usually of a nature where productivity gains cannot easily be used to offset upwards pressure on costs, as can happen in the kind of economic activity more typical of the private sector. Thus the relative cost of public services tends to rise disproportionately. To control this, governments are tempted to undervalue the public service ethos and overvalue efficiency, leading to a deterioration both in the services delivered and in the culture of public service.

A further threat to the productive functioning of a market economy comes from the attempt to squeeze too much out for socially desirable ends. This can begin to bear down on economic growth and lead to stagnation or even recession. It discourages innovation and enterprise, and eventually the tap of ever-increasing prosperity is turned off. Such has been the fate of various Western European economies in the last decade, though the evidence suggests the British and Irish economies have avoided that mistake. Their restraint translates as political pressure to spend more and to redistribute a greater share of national income to those at the lower end of the scale. It is hotly disputed as to how much of this pressure market economies can bear before their performance is adversely affected.

COMPETITION, INEQUALITY AND RISK

Even a well regulated labour market may produce an unjustified degree of inequality

Even a well regulated labour market may produce a degree of inequality widely seen as unjustified. Hence active steps may have to be taken to correct a tendency to increase inequality, taking account of political and economic judgements as to what degree of inequality the common good will tolerate before it suffers damage.

Active steps may have to be taken to correct a tendency to increase inequality

Such judgements will combine subjective and objective factors. Few members of Western societies today suffer the abject poverty that would have been familiar a century ago. Social scientists have tended therefore to use a relative rather than an absolute definition of poverty. Taking the median income as a bench mark (not the average but the level at which an equal number lies above and below), they have defined poverty as an income at or below 60 per cent of that level. This is the figure used by the Government's own Index of Multiple Deprivation, which does, however, also take into account a wide variety of other factors. By such measures, inequality is increasing. The Henley Centre forecasts that by 2010 the top ten per cent of the UK population will be ten times richer than the bottom ten per cent. But arithmetic can give a misleading impression. Relative poverty is more a measure of inequality and hence of social exclusion than of a lack of access to material goods. When the term poverty is used without qualification or context its meaning is not always clear.

Neither relative nor absolute poverty are wholly adequate concepts to describe what is at stake. For instance if all households ought to be able to afford a television and are entitled to help if they cannot obtain one unaided - which may well be the case - ought all households be helped to afford a computer, for instance, particularly as teachers increasingly rely on students having access to the internet for their studies? Is the inability of a student to access the internet a form of social exclusion? The time may be approaching when it is right to say that it is. Similarly the definition of poverty should take into account the effects of exclusion from cultural activities. The highest artistic achievements of our civilization should be accessible as widely as possible. Thus 'cultural poverty' also deprives people of the right to participate in society.

Establishing a consensus about what a 'decent minimum' might be will require intense public consultation and debate. Inequality and the exclusion it can lead to can cause stress, mental and physical illness, as well as resentment and crime. A prosperous society, in the full moral sense of the term, is not one where certain groups are excluded from participation through poverty, even if that poverty is relative. The assessment of minimum living standards acceptable in a prosperous society would be helped by the creation of an independent statutory body such as a Minimum Income Standards Agency.

As a general principle, it seems to be the case that a dynamic economy, while requiring equality of opportunity,

'Cultural poverty' deprives people of the right to participate in society

Relative poverty is more a measure of inequality and social exclusion than of a lack of access to material goods

Inequality and exclusion can cause stress and mental and physical illness, as well as resentment and crime

Christians concerned for social justice often find the reward of risk problematical

does generate a certain degree of inequality of rewards, so that some individuals have an economic incentive to make exceptional efforts or run exceptional risks. But Christians concerned for social justice often find the reward of risk problematical. This reservation is not always justified. A modern market economy adjusts its financial parameters day by day according to many marginal calculations of probability: will a share price go up or down in the immediate future; will a basket of shares show a gain or loss at the end of a day's trading? Such adjustment mechanisms are necessary, for without them markets would quickly lose touch with reality.

One form of risk-taking readily accommodated into an ethical framework is genuine entrepreneurship, where an individual or group has the courage and vision to set up a new industrial or business enterprise. Often the driving motive will not be financial profit, but the satisfaction of a creative urge to do something that has not been done before or to make something that did not exist before, at the same time meeting human needs and wants. Such entrepreneurship is of great service to the common good, meets humanity's deep need to be inventive and creative, and deserves proper reward. If the entrepreneur gains satisfaction from the risk-taking itself, so be it. Governments rightly welcome such initiative and seek to adjust conditions to foster it. The fact that the enterprise involved risk, and the possibility of loss rather than gain, justifies higher levels of reward because of the creativity, courage, leadership and personal commitment displayed in taking those risks. The inequalities resulting from those higher levels of reward are not always unjust. Nor, however, is it unjust to expect those enjoying higher levels of reward to make a reasonable and fair contribution to the common purse, through taxation. But the level of taxation has to be such that enterprise is not discouraged.

The level of taxation has to be such that enterprise is rewarded

The driving motive of genuine entrepreneurship will not be financial profit, but the satisfaction of a creative urge

The disproportionate rise in top levels of income over the last decade has reopened the debate about higher rates of taxation for higher rates of pay. Those who earn roughly double the average income are already subject to a higher rate of 40 per cent. There is a reasonable case for, say, a higher rate still on those earning three or four times (or some other multiple of) the average income in the interests of social justice; as there is a reasonable case for removing those on half the median income from income tax altogether.

The remuneration of directors has been subject for some years to intense upward pressure, where upward movement in one boardroom or one sector of business or industry is quickly used to justify a knock-on effect elsewhere. Remuneration for managers and executives below board level has also increased disproportionately. Considerations of risk-taking rarely apply, though they are sometimes invoked. But it happens too often that directors or senior managers, far from being rewarded for successful innovation or genuine risk taking, seem to receive what amounts to a reward for failure.

Too often directors or senior managers seem to receive a reward for failure

This is also proving increasingly harmful to industrial relations. It makes almost impossible the cultivation of the creative collaborative or co-operative spirit between employees and employers that Christian social ethics regards as fundamentally important. Ordinary employees resent being offered low single-figure pay rises by managers and directors whose pay is already 40 or 50 or more times larger than their own and who have recently voted each other substantial double-figure increases. This applies equally in relation to pensions.

If directors ignore the need to be seen to act equitably towards their own pay, their industries and businesses will not prosper

If directors ignore the need to be seen to act equitably towards their own pay, their industries and businesses will not prosper. Many shareholders and those who represent them have begun to see these dangers, as well as to sense the underlying moral issues. They have attempted to use their powers (as ultimate owners of the business) to control excessive boardroom packages. Church institutional investors have rightly been active in these areas, but undoubtedly could be more effective. Managers and directors have grown accustomed to being allowed to run business in their own interests rather than the interests of shareholders, though that is usually the alibi they hide behind. Sometimes they have lost sight of the difference. Thus it is right for the Government to review company law to see to what extent shareholders could gain greater control over boardroom pay as well as other aspects of company policy.

Companies should be made more easily answerable to

It is right for the Government to see to what extent shareholders could gain greater control over company policy the common good. In general, a situation where investors are encouraged or allowed to think only about short-term dividends and share-price movements, and not to take any further interest in what is done with their property (as invested capital) as it affects the common good, is not compatible with a Christian ethic of the responsible stewardship of wealth.

Just as attempts by trade unions to control the supply of labour has sometimes begun to show some aspects of monopoly and the consequent distortions of market conditions, so the collusion between highly paid businessmen and company directors to drive up each others' pay has displayed aspects of a cartel, as well as distorting some markets.

Competition generally favours the common good and increases prosperity

Indeed one point of agreement between Adam Smith and Karl Marx was that providers of goods and services do not like competition, but usually prefer to organize themselves into what Smith called 'conspiracies against the public.' While competition generally favours the common good and increases prosperity, conscious or unconscious collusion to defeat competition is harmful to the common good. Governments have a legitimate interest - in defence of the common good - in enforcing competition and breaking up cartels and monopolies.

Conscious or unconscious collusion to defeat competition is harmful to the common good

The public has a particular interest in maintaining competition in broadcasting and the print media, for only by having a diverse range of sources for its information can it have any confidence in what it is being told. Justice cannot be done to some of the hard choices facing society in a market economy if the mass media ignore, trivialize, slant or unduly personalize their coverage of them. The natural market corrective - fewer people will buy newspapers if they no longer trust them - does not meet the need for reliable information. It would merely encourage more and more people to vacate the public space and withdraw from their participation in civil society. One of the main ways in which ordinary citizens participate in the workings of a democracy is through the media, and citizenship is fundamentally diminished if news reporting, particularly the coverage of political issues, is presented primarily as a

Justice cannot be done to the hard choices in society if the mass media ignore, trivialize, slant or unduly personalize its coverage

Citizenship is fundamentally diminished if news reporting is presented primarily as a form of entertainment

form of entertainment. Politicians should not expect to be treated with deference, but are entitled to a fair opportunity for putting across their policies and ideas; and the public has a right to hear them.

RENEWAL OF CIVIL SOCIETY

The voluntary sector, including religious and charitable organizations, relies on a high degree of personal motivation and commitment to the common good. Those whose motivation is not primarily financial should not be disparaged for it; even less should they be accused of disguised self-interest. The renewal of civil society will not be achieved if it is left solely to the profit-motive. The ethos of public service needs cherishing.

Hence the Government's ten year 'National Strategy for Neighbourhood Renewal' will not succeed unless it involves the full participation of central and local government, private, voluntary, faith and community sector organizations. The harnessing of individual effort into effective and empowered local organizations is the creation of a form of wealth called 'social capital.' Economists may neglect it because they find it difficult to measure; Christian social ethicists regard it as priceless. They know that the neighbourhood renewal envisaged in the strategy, through steps ranging from improvements in the urban environment, the control of antisocial behaviour, the creation of a range of shared communal facilities and in general the cultivation of a spirit of 'neighbourliness', are all vital if the quality of life of people living in such neighbourhoods is to be improved. Indeed, prosperity without such improvements would be deeply flawed.

The Churches do not presuppose that it is invariably the duty of the State to relieve the diverse ills of a modern society. Sometimes the State will be the primary agent in doing so, sometimes it will be a facilitator, sometimes a source of funding; but often the best remedies will lie outside the scope of state action altogether. Sometimes the State will even be the cause of the problem. The Churches are well used to playing their part in a vibrant civil society,

The renewal of civil society will not be achieved if it is left solely to the profit motive. The ethos of public service needs cherishing

The harnessing of individual effort into effective and empowered local organizations is the creation of a form of wealth called 'social capital'

Economists may neglect it

Christian social ethicists regard it as priceless

A system of social security available to all was rightly regarded by many at the time as a necessary dimension of a compassionate Christian society

Devolutionary theory has become a key concept in the renewal of political legitimacy

Excessive concentration of power at the centre has become a fertile source of apathy and cynicism

and look to its renewal as an essential element in the service of the common good. They are well placed to take a lead in this, in partnership with all the other elements that constitute the rich social fabric of our communities.

The great insight of William Beveridge, whose work on the foundation principles of the Welfare State owed a good deal to the influence of his close friend Archbishop William Temple, was that only the State could organize a system of social security that was funded by the contributions of the whole community and available to all without distinction. It was rightly regarded by many at the time as a necessary dimension of a compassionate Christian society. As a result there was a tendency to think that it was natural for the State to assume all the responsibilities that had previously been borne by one or other institution in civil society. In so far as those institutions had not proved equal to the task, that was a necessary step forwards.

But measures designed to correct one injustice may sometimes unintentionally create another. The pendulum may sometimes swing too far. The necessity now is to repair the public space - the domain of civil society - so that institutions of all sorts, including religious bodies, can freely and fully participate in the progress of a truly pluralistic society. The common good, the upholding of which is the proper function of such a society, is by no means the exclusive concern of governments; these must, indeed, know where to stop before they invade the rightful space of other agencies and institutions.

This notion of the autonomy of 'intermediate' institutions - standing between the state and the individual - has in the past had strong expression in Christian societies. The doctrine of subsidiarity has become a dominant theme of some systems of social ethics. The term may be less familiar than the concept. British and Irish political experience has looked increasingly warmly towards the theory of devolution, understood not so much as the delegation of supreme power from the top but as the re-ordering of structures of governance - public and private - to bring the making of decisions closer to the people affected by them, thereby increasing their sense of involvement. Devolutionary theory (often related to the concept of subsidiarity) has become a key concept in the revival of political culture and the renewal of political legitimacy, while the opposite, excessive concentration of power at the centre, has become a fertile source of apathy and cynicism.

Devolutionary theory asserts that the right of free institutions within civil society to operate does not depend on government permission. Each agency or institution has an inherent right to exercise the authority proper to itself, which Christians will see as ultimately coming from God. A wrong is done against the common good whenever decision-making is reserved for a higher level of administration than is necessary. Local diversity enriches the community, while centrally imposed uniformity diminishes and demeans it.

Each agency has an inherent right to exercise the authority proper to itself, which Christians see as coming from God

While the building blocks of a renewed civil society are all in place, the relationship between the parts has not kept pace with changing circumstances. Work for the good of the community has traditionally rested on four 'pillars': individual effort, government (local and national), charities (including religious groups) and the private sector. But a proper sense of partnership between the four pillars of care has not yet emerged: they are too often seen as rivals, or one as subordinate to the other.

A renewed civil society would see the restoration of the idea of public service as good in itself

A renewed civil society would see the restoration of the idea of public service as good in itself, and the cherishing of those intermediate institutions which cultivate and preserve ethical and professional standards and hand them on to future generations. Similarly the voluntary sector will take its place as the jewel in the crown of a healthy civil society, it will not be marginalized as a poor relation. This sector, especially its religious element, plays a crucial role in transmitting core moral and social values from one generation to the next. It is able to pioneer new areas of work, particularly those that are unfashionable or unpopular, such as among asylum seekers, sex offenders, drug addicts or those living with HIV-AIDS.

The involvement of religious based institutions in this and similar work is motivated by a desire to serve, rather than a desire simply to proselytize, and any discrimination against them because of their religious basis is unreasonable and unfair.

The four pillars of care - individual effort, government, charities and the private sector - are too often seen as rivals, or one as subordinate to another

The increasing amounts of state or local authority funding that find their way into the voluntary sector

Voluntary bodies would be strengthened by restoring the tax advantages formerly enjoyed by charities on investment income

One of the major priorities of the EU should be the dispersal of power from the centre

No function should be performed by the EU that cannot equally well be performed by member governments

should not be allowed to compromise the distinctiveness, independence, and degree of personal commitment that are among its chief assets. The financial health of voluntary sector bodies, and thus their status as equal rather than subordinate partners alongside statutory agencies, would be strengthened by restoring the tax advantages formerly enjoyed by charities on investment income.

Devolution is driven forwards by the instinctive desire people have for more control over their lives. It is the fear of losing such control as they still have that makes them fear remote and centralized focuses of power such as they accuse the European Union of becoming. While the stated values of the enlarged EU are entirely laudable, its leaders often talk about the need to awaken public interest and involvement in what they do without seeing that genuine devolution is the only way to achieve it. One of the major priorities of the EU should be the dispersal of power from the centre, to an extent that is visible and credible. The EU's commitment to the principle of subsidiarity has yet to make a significant difference to the way it is perceived. Partly this is because of a superficial and biased treatment of such matters in the mass media; partly it reflects reality. No function should be performed by the EU that cannot equally well be performed by member governments; indeed, devolution should hope to bring about a variety of different solutions to similar problems, so national governments may learn from each other's experiences. Similarly, national governments should avoid performing tasks that can equally well be performed by regional or local administrative bodies, or even by local initiative, provided these are democratically answerable.

COMMITMENT TO SOLIDARITY AND THE COMMON GOOD

A Christian reflection on the proper ordering of human society must take as its starting point the intrinsic and equal worth and dignity of every human individual, made in the image of God and redeemed by Christ. Human beings are social animals, and their conduct towards one another has always been regulated by rules for which, traditionally, divine sanction is invoked. As well as duties towards each other as individuals, Christian social ethics has always recognized the duty of an individual to society as a whole, and has made rules for that too. Indeed, no society can flourish without such rules. Ideally they become not rules imposed from without and enforced by sanctions, but the internalized values of a well furnished conscience.

The core of this ethical teaching is the concept of the common good. This has classical roots in Platonic and Aristotelian philosophy, and is a concept familiar to Judaism and Islam. The current understanding of the concept of the common good in Christian theology looks back to the work of Thomas Aquinas, and before that, to Augustine of Hippo.

The concept of the common good differs from more ethically neutral expressions such as 'the public good' because it can contain a moral imperative. The ethical heart of this idea is the need for commitment to one's neighbour, at the level of community as well as of the individual. Entering into this commitment involves entry into a new moral universe, where 'loving God and loving one's neighbour' begins to take precedence over all things. But not all who are committed to the common good would want to describe their commitment in these explicitly Christian terms. It is a characteristic feature of Christian social ethics that Christians working for the common good have been prepared to work with people of goodwill whatever their beliefs.

This change of heart in entering a deep commitment to the common good changes attitudes which determine each person's relationship with neighbours, human communities, and with nature itself: the ordered mutually connected system, including animals, which makes up the natural world. All of these elements are involved in the common good: any communal effort that does not embrace all of them cannot claim that title. The common good is therefore the whole network of social conditions enabling human individuals and groups to flourish and live a fully, genuinely human life, sometimes described as integral human development.

The relationship between the common good and prosperity - understood as 'human prospering' in all its complexity - is obviously very close. Nor is 'human prospering' worthy of the name if some are excluded from

The core of this ethical teaching is the concept of the common good, and is a concept familiar to Judaism and Islam

A new moral universe where 'loving God and loving one's neighbour' begins to take precedence over all things

Christians working for the common good have been prepared to work with people of goodwill whatever their beliefs

35

All are responsible for all the whole human family

it. All are responsible for all, individually and collectively, at the level of society, nation and indeed the whole human family. This must include members of the family as yet unborn, to whom a moral duty exists, so to speak, forward in time.

The concept of the common good is so closely related to the virtue of solidarity that it almost stands part of the definition. When men and women in various parts of the world feel personally afflicted by the injustices and violations of human rights committed in distant countries - which perhaps they will never visit - and when that response is not a feeling of vague or passing sympathy at the misfortunes of others but a firm and persevering recognition of interdependence, there occurs a transformation in moral awareness, a reborn consciousness. The result is the social and moral 'virtue' of solidarity, which integrates into the conscience of the person concerned as an unvarying underlying principle: that all are responsible for all. The virtue of solidarity so-called is an over-arching virtue, to which particular virtues - honesty, integrity, thrift, patience, kindness, courage, modesty and so on - all contribute. They are the practical ways in which one lives out the obligation to 'love your neighbour as yourself.'

'Love of neighbour' and 'love of God' have always been intrinsically linked in Christian thinking

In seeing and accepting the spiritual truth behind the concept of the common good, the individual alters his or her entire orientation towards others. It is the moment when the true humanity and dignity of other people is grasped and internalized - when the individual fully understands for the first time that he or she is not alone. Henceforth any clash of interests between pursuing individual interests and pursuing the common good is dissolved, as the individual sees that his or her true interests can never be served by deterioration in the common good.

The virtue of solidarity is an over arching virtue to which honesty, integrity, thrift, patience, kindness, courage, modesty - all contribute

Whether he or she knows it or not, an individual at such a moment is also turning towards God. 'Love of neighbour' and 'love of God' have always been so intrinsically linked in Christian thinking as to amount to two sides of the same coin. Christ's teaching in the parable of the Good Samaritan shows that the concept of 'neighbour' is not to be confined to 'people like us' but to extend to the whole human race.

There are no exceptions to those we are to love, not even our 'enemies'.

Despite the Christian perception that the concept of the common good has these profound religious implications, the concept is itself well understood from within other traditions, and indeed, from a secular philosophical standpoint too. As well as a tendency towards self-interest, there is a deep well of altruism in human nature. It is seen to run with the grain of what it means to be a human being, who is a social and not a solitary animal. The converse, the individual who has no regard for the rights or interests of others, offends the moral sensibility of humanity as a whole.

PROSPERITY AND DEVOLUTION

If the only factors to be considered were the advance of the common good and the virtue of solidarity, there would be a danger that states might arrogate to themselves a task which is in fact the duty of every citizen. Benign dictators (or those claiming to be benign) do indeed frequently claim to be pursuing the common good on behalf of their people, and indeed to know better than their people where their true interests lie. That is why the theory of devolution is a necessary corrective, for it puts a moral duty on the State not to usurp the proper functioning of other bodies in society. It is therefore an effective antidote to a range of possible distortions in the structuring of societies, including dictatorships and over-centralized so-called command economies, and the undue aggrandizement of the State itself.

A healthy society will be one where devolutionary theory is fully respected, including the proper autonomy of family life. It is also a necessary condition for a successful culture of economic enterprise. As well as fostering the functioning of intermediate institutions and agencies independent of the state, this theory enriches freedom and democracy and encourages participation at all levels including those which most affect people's lives. The lack of effective devolution is a powerful factor leading to political alienation and apathy; the 'retreat from community' is one of the causes of isolation and anxiety.

As well as a tendency to self interest, there is a deep well of altruism in human nature

The concept of neighbour is not to be confined to 'people like us', but to extend to the whole human race

A healthy society will be one where devolutionary theory is fully respected

The lack of effective devolution is a powerful factor leading to political alienation and apathy

*Responsible citizenship
and voluntary action are
the essential elements in a
properly functioning civil
society*

The ideas the devolutionary theory of subsidiarity conveys are entirely familiar in our context. National, regional and local government and the presence of what Edmund Burke called the 'Little Platoons' are the fundamental constituents of society, indicating a long and strong tradition of responsible citizenship and voluntary action. These are essential elements in a properly functioning civil society, which together make up the common good.

*The 'retreat from
community' is one of the
causes of isolation and
anxiety*

The popular demand to be governed nearer home has expressed itself in significant devolutionary reform of the constitution of the United Kingdom in recent years; a story not yet finished. The Parliament in Scotland now enjoys a wide degree of autonomy, including powers of law-making. The Assembly in Wales has fewer devolved powers, but there is a live issue as to how and whether these should be extended. Devolution in Northern Ireland has been held back by political differences, but there is no desire to see the instruments of devolution dismantled. The Republic of Ireland is an independent nation state, although constrained by its membership of the European Union and by its heavy exposure to the global market. But the struggle for Irish independence from Britain could be characterized as driven by a strong urge for freedom, self-determination, and national pride - factors also present in the other 'nationalisms' and assertions of identity in these islands to which devolution has been the response.

*Different national and
regional experiences
confirm that the sense of
prosperity is not always
solely determined by
economic factors*

Different national and regional experiences confirm that the sense of prosperity is not always solely determined by economic factors. Northern Ireland, Scotland, Wales and the English North West are relatively poor areas by comparison with the average. Yet, given a reasonable and secure income, the quality of life enjoyed there is often enviable. The benefits of cleaner air, emptier roads, a wider range of affordable choices and a more manageable pace of life create levels of well-being that constitute genuine prosperity.

But the experience of the less fortunate can be dramatically different. Scotland, for instance, suffers a higher concentration of poverty, long-term unemployment, sickness and disability than the rest of the United Kingdom. There is still a 'stubborn refusal' of poverty to respond to policies designed to defeat it. More is spent on health care than in the rest of the UK, but health is worse. Inward investment is dwindling, and business start-up rates are too low to create the necessary number of new jobs. The population is declining and ageing; arguably, Scottish society would benefit from a relaxation of UK immigration policy, not least to bolster the number of people of working age to balance the increasing number of those who have retired.

Nevertheless the nation has great strengths. The Scottish Churches have made a strong plea that poor communities should be given the resources to solve their own problems, and the culture of community regeneration is an increasingly vigorous one. It is strongly felt that greater economic autonomy is needed to address distinctively Scottish problems of poverty. However, unease is registered by the extent to which the industrial economy of Scotland - as indeed elsewhere in the United Kingdom - is dependent on armaments. Britain's prominence in the international arms trade, while a source of jobs and economic growth, is a particular challenge to the Christian conscience.

In Wales, the hope of wider prosperity tends to come up against obstinate social and economic realities. Welsh income levels are below the UK average, though the quality of life, when not measured purely by economic factors, is often subjectively higher. This is an important reminder that contentment and peace of mind are not consumer goods that can be bought and sold, but depend on cultural and spiritual factors that need careful nurturing. In this spirit the Welsh Assembly has sought to recognize the great variety of Welsh identities and cultures.

The policy of combating poverty by getting people into work is running into difficulties in Wales just as in other old industrial heartlands. Many workers with advanced skills once in demand in traditional industries lack the necessary qualifications to find equivalent work in new industries. Some of the available jobs there are not well paid or highly skilled, and low pay can still leave people in poverty. Such jobs are at risk as employers can move to countries

Britain's prominence in the international arms trade is a particular challenge to the Christian conscience

Greater economic autonomy is needed to address distinctively Scottish problems of poverty

Welsh income levels are below the UK average, though the quality of life is often subjectively higher

39

Improving the quality of work needs a revival of community and civic life in a healthy partnership

An increasing role for the churches and faith communities engaged in a wide range of successful and sustainable community activity

Taxation in the Republic accounts for a lower proportion of national income than anywhere else in the EU

The question of social justice remains deeply controversial

where wage rates are even lower. Improving the quality of work, and therefore the level of wages, will require the raising of education standards and an expansion in training and retraining in vocational skills. This cannot be left to government, whether in Cardiff or in Westminster, but needs a revival of community and civic life in a healthy partnership between local authorities, the private and voluntary sectors, and churches and faith communities.

The experience of the North West Region reinforces this general impression. As in Wales, incomes in the Region are below the average UK level. Similarly, the gateway to prosperity seems barred to many people. Compared to the UK average, people are less educated, less well trained, more subject to ill-health and more likely to be on disability income. Though unemployment has declined, the numbers of those in poorly-paid work has increased. As elsewhere, however, there is a revival of community spirit and a reappraisal of the contribution that civil society makes to public life. This has resulted in an increasing role for churches and faith communities, which are engaged in a wide range of successful and sustainable community activity.

This project has drawn material from both the Republic and from Northern Ireland, through the good offices of the Department of Social Issues of the Irish Council of Churches. The differences are dramatic, and were illustrated in two seminars, one in Dublin and one in Belfast.

The Republic has made extraordinary economic advances since entry into the European Union in 1972. Its vigorous efforts to attract inward investment have been largely successful. One part of that investor-friendly strategy has been to keep corporate and personal taxes low. As a result, taxation in the Republic accounts for a much lower proportion of national income than anywhere else in the EU. So those who have not shared in the proceeds of the boom are not compensated for their poverty in anything like the standard European fashion. The Churches first raised the issue of prosperity and its purposes in the Republic, and the question of social justice remains deeply controversial.

40

Northern Ireland, like Scotland and Wales, has experienced serious economic hardship as old industries declined. But thirty years of conflict have also inflicted much serious damage on the well being of the people. This has been a much less favoured destination for external investment, for several reasons, and it is among the most slowly developing regions of the EU. Northern Ireland enjoys its current prosperity as a result of decisions on increased public expenditure taken in Westminster. But the consequent expansion in public sector employment is squeezing out the private sector, thus reducing the capacity to foster that kind of competitive innovation fundamental to wealth creation and sustained prosperity.

Northern Ireland enjoys its current prosperity as a result of decisions on increased public expenditure taken in Westminster

Ireland - North and South - well illustrates the conundrum of prosperity across Europe: fastest growth is often achieved by countries with the least generous social provision, while economies where the state's share of the gross national product is highest, largely to finance generous state benefits, are among the most stagnant. The secret of successful European politics - to optimize both economic growth and social justice - is proving elusive. British satisfaction that it has found the right balance seems premature in the light of the persistence of poverty in Scotland, Wales, the North of England, London, the South West, and other regions.

The conundrum of prosperity across Europe: fastest growth is often achieved by countries with the least generous social provision, while economies where the state's share of the gross national product is highest are among the most stagnant

WORK AS COLLABORATION IN GOD'S CREATION

Christian social ethics has something else to say about work. It does not regard the relative economic rewards of one form of work compared with another as a true measure of the moral value of their contribution to the common good. Christians will be careful, therefore, not to base esteem for one form of work compared with another on the amount of pay received for it, or indeed, whether there is payment involved at all. To use an obvious example, few roles are more valuable to the community than the loving care and proper upbringing of young children by their parents. By the values of the kingdom of God, such work should be held in high esteem, but because it is not paid work; society can easily make the mistake of undervaluing it.

Christians will be careful not to base esteem for one form of work compared with another as a true measure of the moral value of their contribution to the common good

41

Through work we do not simply make more, we become more

Human work is properly seen through Christian eyes as continuing the original work of creation. The story of Genesis teaches us how God, having made the world 'in six days', then handed over the created world to the care of humanity. Just as God's original creative work made order out of chaos, so humanity's calling is to make more order yet. In this respect the vocation to work creatively, in imitation of and in co-operation with God's creativity, is an aspect of the doctrine that human beings are made in the image of God. This has important implications for a Christian ethic of work. Genesis also records the story of the Fall, which has sometimes been interpreted as suggesting that the need to work was a collective punishment for humanity's disobedience. Instead, it is right to view work less as a constraint or discipline, more as an opportunity to express our freedom and human creativity and to participate in the sustaining creative power of God. Through work, we do not simply make more, we become more. Even the hardships of work can have a spiritual and liberating meaning. It is not surprising, therefore, that many popular forms of leisure activity, including sport and various hobbies, do in fact have many of the attributes of hard work even when they are not financially rewarded.

What God did originally in bringing order out of chaos has a constant tendency to unravel

It is a scientific insight that organized systems always tend to decay into disorganized systems (the Second Law of Thermodynamics), so what God did originally in bringing order out of chaos has a constant tendency to unravel, to return to chaos. One of the chief functions of work is therefore in the continuous repair of the created order, holding chaos (entropy) at bay. But it also consists in bringing new things into being, new patterns of order. That process can refer both to goods and to services. An increase in goods and services available to the community or to individuals may be described as an increase in wealth. So human work is closely connected to wealth creation, even before it is subject to economic measurement.

The dehumanization of work by turning it into soulless drudgery is contrary to God's design for humanity

Work needs to preserve its God-given character as an activity worthy of humans made in the image of God. The dehumanization of work, by turning it into soulless drudgery, is unacceptable and contrary to God's design for humanity. At the same time the creative instinct ennobles work, because it brings it closer to God's intentions. It follows that

The creative instinct ennobles work, because it brings it closer to God's intentions

a Christian ethic of work will seek to maximize the dignity of work by maximising creative input. Thus it enriches the common good.

Those whose work is to manage the work of others should see that the work is structured in a way that does justice to these principles. Individual workers need to be given an optimum degree of control of their work environment, so they can see and understand the purpose of what they do, co-operate with others on a basis of mutual respect, apply their skills and training, contribute thoughtfully to adaptations and developments, feel responsibility for the quality of their work, and take pride in the outcome. In return they are entitled to fair reward, and to the respect and satisfaction that belongs to someone who is fulfilling a divine vocation. They are also entitled to join with others in trade associations and unions for the protection of their individual and collective rights and interests. All this gives them a sense of 'ownership' of their 'good work', the opposite of a worker's sense of alienation from his or her labour which has been one of the major defects of the industrialized work environment and a source of industrial conflict.

If these conditions are met, workers are offered the opportunity of feeling they are co-operating with owners and managers in the important task of wealth creation rather than fighting over the spoils of their labour and in perpetual conflict with their overseers. Owners and managers in turn will see the ethical case for such a way of conducting work going with the grain of human nature rather than against it, in accordance with God's design. Furthermore, economic theory predicts that a well-trained and motivated workforce constitutes a form of capital - 'human capital' - which is vital to the success of any economic enterprise. The liberation of the creative energy of such a workforce can transform its effectiveness. Well-founded economic growth is the outcome. The blocking of creative energy, on the other hand, leads to frustration, apathy and resentment.

A Christian ethic of work, recognising the vocational character of all work and the spark of the divine in it, must reject any general depiction of labour as merely an exploitable commodity, or workers as naturally work-shy

God's design is going with the grain of human nature rather than against it

The liberation of the creative energy of the workforce can transform its effectiveness

The blocking of creative energy on the other hand, leads to frustration, apathy and resentment

Unemployment is not only wasteful but contrary to God's design

To work is a right and to deprive someone of work an injustice

43

or lazy. Unemployment is not only wasteful, but contrary to God's design. People want to work, provided the work available to them is good work. Governments have a responsibility to minimize unemployment, and to encourage the labour market to match skills to jobs. It also follows that to work is a right and to deprive someone of work is an injustice. In a rapidly changing world, however, it does not follow that any particular worker has a right to pursue any particular trade, or indeed stay with a particular employer, for his or her lifetime. But society should recognize that a change of work is a time of vulnerability, and that redundancy payments, the protection of pension rights and access to any required retraining are necessary to recognize and value the contribution a worker has made.

Rates of remuneration will necessarily be influenced by market conditions, taking into account factors already mentioned such as scarcity and degree of skill required. But ethical considerations would forbid rates that are so low as to amount to exploitation. The minimum wage is an acceptable device for preventing this, and to minimize the possibility of exploitation it should be set as high as possible without acting as a disincentive to full employment. The exploitation signalled by low wages is usually an indication that a particular type of work ought to be regarded as wrongly designed and economically inefficient, and the tasks it covers would be better achieved in alternative ways. The minimum wage can therefore be used as a way of ensuring that all forms of work available are worthwhile.

Nevertheless some of those in work will not earn enough to escape from poverty, especially if they have the responsibility of supporting a family. Where wages fall below the required level, it will sometimes be necessary for the state to intervene with supplementary payments, in order to raise the level of income to a 'living wage' for that person in those circumstances. In this sense Christian social ethics recognizes the 'right to a living wage' as a right that can be met jointly by an employer and by the state. The recognition of such a right should remove any demeaning sense that state benefits paid for this purpose are discretionary or optional, or something for which an individual has to beg. They are an entitlement, and the State has a duty to ensure that access to this entitlement is made as easy as possible, with due respect for individual dignity. Excessive bureaucracy in the administration of such benefits actually stands in the way of individuals exercising their right to a living wage, and should be avoided.

Ethical considerations also apply when an employee has other important responsibilities which can sometimes conflict with work responsibilities. This group includes those who care for others – the elderly and the disabled, but especially those who are parents of children. The life-work balance will not be correctly set if the care of children is undervalued, or if such responsibilities are seen simply as a lifestyle choice made for selfish reasons. A Christian social ethic will treat the raising of children as one of the most important ways individuals can contribute to the common good, not only because of the needs of the children themselves when young but because of the value to the community of happy and well-adjusted adults once they grow up - including their economic value to the future workforce. Even in the world of work, therefore, Christians will want to emphasize the importance of family life and make room for its demands. Those, particularly women, who shoulder these dual responsibilities, must be protected from unfair discrimination in pay, promotion, conditions of work and pension arrangements, or any diminution in professional esteem. And it is reasonable for them to look to society for the help they need, financial and otherwise, to make their family and work roles compatible. The balance between family commitments and work commitments should be renegotiable between employees and employers. Increasingly employees will exercise the right to choose the balance that suits them and their families, as more people forego the maximization of income in return for other less material rewards and satisfactions.

The responsibility of fathers must be recognized in their working conditions. Where they are solely responsible for the care of children, the same consideration should apply as to mothers. But employers have no right to insist that any particular distribution of parental roles should apply in the families of those they employ, so whoever wishes to act as the principal carer may do so. Even when a parent is not the principal carer of the children, employers should respect his or her right to a personal and family life, which includes

A Christian social ethic will treat the raising of children as one of the most important ways individuals can contribute to the common good

The balance between family commitments and work commitments should be renegotiable

The responsibility of fathers must be recognized in their working conditions

45

The employment culture which judges employees by their willingness to work excessive hours is harmful to personal and family life and therefore contrary to a Christian ethic of work

The Welfare State, the state education System and the National Health Service were the three most important legacies of their time

They constitute the principal terms of a new social contract that has characterized this society ever since

having the time and energy for it. Except as a short-term necessity, the employment culture which judges employees by their willingness to work excessive hours is harmful to personal and family life and therefore contrary to a Christian ethic of work.

While safeguarding the interests of parents, however, it would be seriously wrong to neglect the interests of young children. The government strategy of attacking poverty by reducing unemployment can result in women with small children being forced back into work sooner than they might otherwise wish, or than the interests of those children might dictate. The evidence of numerous surveys appears to suggest that below the age of three, children do not always thrive in childcare facilities, but may well do so from then on. The availability of government assistance with the cost of childcare has produced an incentive for women to pay other women to look after their children of whatever age instead of doing so themselves (for which, of course, they would not be paid).

WORK AS THE ANSWER TO POVERTY

Beveridge's proposed reforms of the social insurance system were closely related to economic deprivation. With the Depression still a recent memory, the obvious source of deprivation at that time was unemployment, caused by a collapse in the world economy. Society as a whole, through universal contributions to social insurance, would share the cost of unemployment so that the load did not fall excessively on one disadvantaged group, the unemployed and their dependants. Society would share the financial burden of sickness, so that falling ill would no longer automatically threaten a working man and his family with ruin. Similarly, an adequate retirement pension would be provided. Society was also to share the cost of educating the young and treating the sick. The Welfare State, the state education system and the National Health Service were the three most important legacies of that time, and they constitute the principal terms of a new social contract between individuals and the State that has characterized this society ever since.

However, efforts to relieve hardship can often create

unexpected problems. Payments to relieve the poverty of the unemployed can be subtly transformed over time into unintentional and 'perverse' incentives to become, or stay, unemployed. The undermining of self-confidence and the willingness to work becomes, in due time, a cause of unemployment in itself. A better trained, more flexible and well-motivated workforce provides business and industry with what it needs to expand. Provided the Government has produced an economic climate in which expansion can occur, new jobs will appear, often more highly skilled and therefore better paid than the jobs lost. This form of growth is generated spontaneously within the economy when conditions are suitable. The responsibility of government then is to see that they are. In such circumstances, adding more people to the total labour force does not increase the total out of work, but the total in work. Improvements in productivity, far from causing unemployment, may actually reduce it because of the economic growth that results.

It is on this basis that the current Labour Government has chosen to tackle two threats to national prosperity; economic stagnation and long-term unemployment. It has identified worklessness as a major factor behind poverty of all sorts, especially child poverty and poverty within young families. Permanent unemployment benefit has been replaced with 'job seekers allowance', designed not as a permanent substitute for income from paid work but to tide individuals over while they find their next job. The Government has identified women with children, especially single women, as a group likely to be impoverished and therefore requiring special attention if it is to be helped into work. The same is true of disabled people, who are seen as capable of work as long as the nature of the work is appropriate to their abilities. In addition, certain geographical regions may have special difficulties in developing new forms of employment to replace the old, because new industries and businesses have been slow to respond to the stimuli that governments, national and local, have tried to provide. Essentially, though, the Government's strategy for dealing with poverty relies heavily on cutting unemployment and reducing the effect of perverse incentives, which in turn benefit the economy.

As a buttress to this strategy, the Government has

Improvements in productivity, far from causing unemployment, may actually reduce it because of the economic growth that results

The Government's strategy for dealing with poverty relies heavily on cutting unemployment and reducing the effect of perverse incentives, which in turn benefit the economy

The undermining of self-confidence and the willingness to work becomes a cause of unemployment in itself

modified the tax system, via 'tax credits', to give assistance to people in work who do not have enough to live on or to support a family. This puts an increased reliance on means testing, to assess the shortfall between needs and resources. This leads inevitably to the 'benefits trap' or 'poverty trap' - an individual quickly discovers that earning extra money results in a corresponding tapering off of benefits or credits. The trap is compounded when several different kinds of benefit designed to relieve poverty - for instance free school meals and housing benefit as well as credits paid to supplement income - are all means-tested. This has an effect similar to a high marginal rate of taxation, sometimes above 50 per cent, occasionally approaching 90 per cent. This is manifestly undesirable. Thus the Government's anti-poverty strategy of encouraging paid work has built-in limits to its effectiveness, both in relieving poverty itself and in producing a fairer society.

This indicates that a wider spread of policies is needed than the present focus on employment as the only effective answer to poverty. Those who are most income-deprived are usually also deprived of credit (except on grossly exploitative terms) and of capital, and those obstacles are equally marks of poverty. Rates of interest, especially to the poor, ought to be subject to a ceiling; and forms of credit suitable for people with low incomes, such as credit unions, should be encouraged with strong government backing. High street lenders such as banks should be reminded of their social responsibility to provide a reasonable service to the less-well-off.

Many more families living in poverty now pay income tax than did so 20 years ago. It is unfair to tax those who manifestly do not have enough money to live on. If poverty is defined as a level of income at or below 60 per cent of the median wage, then that level could reasonably be set as the level below which individuals should not be required to pay any income tax at all. In any event they contribute to the public purse through other forms of taxation such as VAT on goods and services; and they are liable to pay national insurance.

It is for such reasons that, despite good intentions,

government efforts to cut levels of poverty have not been as successful as was desired. 'Income deprivation' is particularly acute in the North East and North West of England, and parts of Wales, Scotland and Northern Ireland. Elsewhere, including several inner London boroughs, unemployment remains relatively severe. This suggests that an employment-based assault on poverty needs to be supported with other measures. Cornwall stands alongside Wales and South Yorkshire as among the poorest regions of Europe, and it would be misleading to divide the entire country into south and north, prosperous and poor.

The 'stubborn refusal' of poverty to respond to the measures designed to relieve it

Nevertheless the total incomes (including benefits and credits) of families with children are rising and the overall number of children in poverty is falling. All parties welcome this, and credit should be given where it is due. But at the same time, from the nations and regions of these islands there is now perplexed talk of the 'stubborn refusal' of poverty to respond to measures designed to relieve it. Existing policies seem to be running into their inherent difficulties, and a complete review of the national anti-poverty strategy has become due. As far as is possible, such policy reviews should be conducted on a cross-party basis, by an independent body of high standing such as the Minimum Income Standards Agency already suggested.

A complete review of the national anti-poverty strategy has become due

One alternative to means-testing is to pay social security entitlements irrespective of income. Strong arguments have been made that this is the answer to one of the most intractable problems of persistent poverty; that afflicting retired people. Since 1979 the basic old age pension has only risen year by year in line with inflation (RPI). The basic pension offers a pensioner little more than the necessities, and an uncomfortable life of financial insecurity and anxiety. Average incomes, meanwhile, have continued to rise faster than the rate of inflation. Successive governments have relied on second pensions, and more recently on 'minimum income guarantees' and 'pensioner credits' - forms of benefit designed to augment the basic pension so it can support a reasonable living standard. To avoid the extra cost of paying those who do not need them, they have been means tested. The Government's stated intention is that the total income of pensioners - basic pension plus these supplementary benefits - will indeed keep pace with average earnings.

One alternative to means-testing is to pay social security entitlements irrespective of income

The basic pension offers a pensioner little more than an uncomfortable life of financial insecurity and anxiety

The Government's intention is that the total income of pensioners will keep pace with average earnings

For various reasons, however, take-up of such benefits has been far from complete. In explanation, some cite the complexity of the means-testing process, some the indignity of it; some a culture that brands discretionary or means-tested entitlements as 'charity'. In any event the Government admits that the availability of these benefits is not sufficiently well known among the target population, especially the very elderly. It seems unlikely that increased efforts to target the relevant groups will have more than a marginal impact, and as a result many retired people will continue to struggle on very low incomes.

The argument of principle for restoring the connection with average incomes rather than the rate of inflation is that retired people should as a matter of justice be entitled to share automatically in the growth of national prosperity - and that they should not have to submit to a means test in order to do so. The pragmatic argument is that only a universal entitlement will reach 100 per cent of the eligible population. On the other hand it is argued that the future cost of incurring universal provision would be unaffordable without hefty tax or national insurance increases (despite savings from no longer administering the means test), and the aim of raising the incomes of the poorest pensioners could be achieved at much lower cost by means-tested benefits. One more easily affordable compromise would be to abolish the means test over the age of 75, and thus pay the full pensioner credit to the category that includes most pensioners in poverty.

The reliance on means testing weakens or destroys the incentive to save for retirement during one's working life. Means tested benefit payments are tapered off to compensate for extra savings or additional pension income, an effect that feels to those affected by it like the unfair penalization of past thrift. These are powerful factors that have to be balanced. Were the Government to agree with the suggestion to set up a Minimum Income Standards Agency with a brief to advise on the eradication of poverty, this would be an issue to be urgently addressed.

Nor is alarm about the plight of pensioners confined to the state sector. In view of the 'black hole' in many pension funds, a review of the tax they pay (especially since the ending of dividend tax credit) is overdue. The present declining rate of take-up of company pensions, and the disappointing performance of such schemes, makes an adequate state-guaranteed pension - however funded - all the more necessary in the fight against pensioner poverty in years to come.

An adequate state-guaranteed pension – however funded – will be all the more necessary in the fight against pensioner poverty in years to come

GLOBAL PROSPERITY AND THE ENVIRONMENT

The ending of poverty throughout the world is a goal to which the human race has not yet adequately committed itself. But there are promising signs. When the New Partnership for Africa's Development (NEPAD) was set up in 2001, it announced its first objective as 'the eradication of poverty' throughout Africa. This African-led initiative, which received strong Western support, went on to commit itself 'to place African countries, both individually and collectively, on a path of sustainable growth and development.' And the way to do this, contained in its third policy objective, was 'to halt the marginalization of Africa in the globalization process and enhance its full and beneficial integration into the global economy.'

The ending of poverty throughout the world is a goal to which the human race has not yet adequately committed itself

Thus economic globalization and the eradication of poverty are intimately linked. All the powerful and rich nations of the world have seen the connection, as have India and China. Nevertheless, the most familiar experience of globalization among the poor people of the world so far has been a decline, not an improvement, in their condition. Clearly globalization is not a good in itself. It could lead to shared global prosperity, or otherwise to further exploitation and division.

One rapid consequence of globalization has been the tendency for cities of the developing world to become focal points or nodes of enterprise, creating a newly enriched class who enjoy unaccustomed prosperity while attracting large numbers of the poor seeking 'crumbs from the rich man's table'. Such cities rapidly display the extremes of wealth and poverty side by side.

Economic globalization and the eradication of poverty are intimately linked

The basic criterion for evaluating the process of

Humanity consists of one global family ... each responsible for each, all with equal rights to access the goods of creation

Globalization as an opportunity to increase economic strength is unacceptable, a structure of sin

The moral case for contributing a greater share of national wealth to the relief of poverty overseas is a compelling one

Trade liberalization should not enforce a dogma but help the poor

economic globalization is: how far does it help to strengthen and reinforce the primary global reality - that humanity consists of one global human family, of which all are members, each responsible for each, all with equal rights to access the goods of creation? Yet the biggest players in the global economy, such as the United States and the European Union, have tended to regard globalization as an opportunity to increase their economic strength, rather than to put it at the service of the global common good. This view is utterly unacceptable and could properly be called a 'structure of sin'; those with the responsibility to promote Christians must throw their full weight into this crucial argument. In particular they have to point out that the achievement of economic growth is by itself no guarantee of an absence of conflict, either internally or between nations, and growth gained unjustly can be a great threat to peace.

Yet the choice facing the wealthier countries is not strictly between one and the other. The politics of globalization are well suited to William Temple's famous dictum that 'public life should be so ordered that self-interest serves what social justice requires.' To regard the advance of prosperity in less developed countries as necessarily being at the expense of living standards in developed countries is misleading. Organized with proper regard to the common good, the relationship could be economically beneficial on both sides. Even if not, the moral case for contributing a greater share of national wealth to the relief of poverty overseas is a compelling one. There is a strong case, therefore, for the United Kingdom and other developed countries to move to implement at long last the UN's standing target of 0.7 per cent of GNP devoted to international aid and development. As demand was stimulated in developing countries, trade flow would increase in both directions, serving both self-interest and justice.

In the short and long term, however, there would be pain as well as gain. This is particularly true when developed countries apply the logic of globalization to their own economies by, for instance, opening domestic markets to goods from the developing world, which may compete with more expensive goods produced locally. But producers in rich countries who cannot exist without protection or subsidy are ultimately in the wrong business. Their predicament results from the way national economic activity has been shaped over past decades, with reference only to the good of the particular nation-state and those within it, and without regard to the ethical requirements of the global common good. On the other hand, temporary protective barriers need not be removed when they shield small, fragile economies in poor countries. Trade liberalization should not enforce a dogma, but help the poor. Christians should be at the forefront of those who understand that the principles of solidarity and the common good - that 'all are responsible for all' - extend beyond national boundaries to embrace every human being.

In the light of this, it is an anomaly that while national institutions have been created to regulate and scrutinize the performance of national markets, the development of equivalent international institutions to regulate international markets has lagged behind. This leaves some of the world's poorest and most vulnerable people open to great hardship and injustice. The World Bank and the International Monetary Fund should see their role not as agents of economic growth at all cost, but as instruments for the promotion of social justice and ecological sustainability on a global scale. The World Trade Organization has the potential to become such an institution. Methods for the regulation of global capital flows, which can sometimes prove critically damaging to weak national economies, need urgent investigation.

It is wrong, furthermore, for those in one part of the world to harm those in another, deliberately, or by neglect or ignorance. Yet that is the fate of the likely victims of global warming, as it leads to rising sea levels and more turbulent and destructive atmospheric conditions. Humanity's ability to alter the whole climate by the discharge of waste gases is a new fact of life, and a world political system based on competing national interests obviously cannot begin to cope with it. The world has to take responsibility for the world.

The pretence that there is no problem is grossly irresponsible and unethical. Economic conditions have to be reshaped in order to deal with global warming, and while much has been achieved by the Kyoto Agreement on

The World Bank and the International Monetary Fund should see their role as instruments for the promotion of social and ecological sustainability on a global scale

Humanity's ability to alter the whole climate by the discharge of waste gases is a new fact of life

The pretence that there is no problem is grossly irresponsible and unethical

53

Governments need to encourage long term research and development on clean and safe alternatives to fossil fuels

emissions-trading, the problem calls for a far more radical and more equitable sharing of emission costs. The principal culprit is the use of fossil fuels as a source of energy for power generation and for transport. Industrial civilization has to find ways of ending its reliance on these, for instance by the systematic and long-term raising of carbon fuel taxation; and the world community has to find ways of encouraging and enforcing them.

It has to do so in ways that do not unfairly penalize less developed nations. They cannot be told that they are forbidden to industrialize or modernize because they may no longer use the energy sources that wealthier counties used when they were developing. However, as their economic development is now clearly seen to be in the interests of the wealthier countries too, the latter have an interest in finding sources of energy that do not damage the environment, and sharing that information with all who need it. Governments, in partnership with industry and with academic scientists, need to encourage long-term research and development on clean and safe alternatives to fossil fuels, and in the meantime, on cleaner ways of using such fuels to produce energy.

Less developed nations cannot be told they are forbidden to industrialize or modernize

Climate change has brought about a revolution in the way people see their responsibilities to the natural world. The image of planet Earth photographed from deep space - humanity's beautiful, vulnerable, unique planetary home - has underlined the precariousness of the eco-system that supports life on this planet. Its apparent tranquillity is easily destabilized; it is by no means impossible for it to become hostile to human life. Nature has been generous so far in providing the conditions for life to exist. But science can offer no guarantee that that generosity will continue, and religion can only offer a warning that it may not.

The Churches must cultivate a religious sense of humility and awe towards the natural world

The Churches now regard it as one of their prime tasks to cultivate a religious sense of humility and awe towards the natural world, to replace the exploitative culture of previous generations that Christianity itself was mistakenly thought to sanction. This transformation of consciousness, an aspect of conversion to the common good previously discussed, would change the political context in which politicians and

54

scientists address these issues, and make possible some of the far-reaching changes in lifestyle and culture that will be necessary if the planet is to be saved.

Prosperity gained at the expense of the habitability of the planet would be a perverse result indeed. Unless human development is sustainable, it is self-defeating. Thus one of the greatest of all the problems that the human race faces is both a product of the pursuit of prosperity and a dire threat to all its hopes and achievements. The human race is unlikely to overcome such threats unless it learns how God intends it to live, and starts to reconstruct its world accordingly - in peace and harmony, in social justice, in humility and in faith.

Unless human development is sustainable, it is self defeating

The human race must learn how God intends it to live and reconstruct its world accordingly in social justice, humility and faith

Acknowledgements

Warmest thanks are due to the *Prosperity with a Purpose* Editorial Group:

David Skidmore   Project Moderator

Simon Best   Merchant Banker

Andrew Britton   Former Executive Secretary 'Unemployment and the Future of Work'

John Ellis   The Methodist Church

Christopher Jones   Church of England

John Kennedy   CTBI

Jonathan Lomax   The Salvation Army

Ian Linden   Former Director, Catholic Institute for International Relations

Charles Wookey   Catholic Bishops' Conference of England and Wales

Thanks are also due to:
The CTBI Church Representatives' Meeting
and to:
Clifford Longley, author of
Prosperity with a Purpose: Christians and the Ethics of Affluence

If you'd like to order more copies of this or the companion volume of essays (*Prosperity with a Purpose: Exploring the Ethics of Affluence*) please use the form on p. 60, or order by phone: CTBI publications 01733 325002 or from the internet:www.ctbi.org.uk/pwap

We hope you have enjoyed reading *Prosperity with a Purpose: Christians and the Ethics of Affluence*. Please join us in debate on these issues at www.ctbi.org.uk/pwap where you'll find a forum for further discussion.

You may also be interested in *Prosperity with a Purpose: Exploring the Ethics of Affluence* (details on page 61) – a collection of essays by Christian thinkers forming part of the Prosperity with a Purpose editorial group. The essays explore the questions raised by this topic in more depth and end with far-reaching policy recommendations.

To order copies of these books please complete the order form overleaf, detach and send to:

CTBI Publications
4 John Wesley Road
Werrington
Peterborough
PE4 6ZP

Or telephone: 01733 325002
Fax: 01733 384180

Or order from our website, www.ctbi.org.uk/pwap

Ordering more than 10 copies of either book will entitle you to
a discount. Please contact us for more details at the address above.

Order Form

I would like to order ……….. copies of
Prosperity with a Purpose: Christians and the Ethics of Affluence – A4
(blue product code CT155)
ISBN 085169 310 5 price £3.99

I would like to order ………. copies of
Prosperity with a Purpose: Exploring the Ethics of Affluence – the
essays (red product code CT156)
ISBN 085169 309 1 price £11.99

*(Please include postage and packing at £1.50 if order total is less than
£5, £3 if total is more than £5. If you live outside the UK we will advise
you of the cost before sending your order.)*

Order total: plus p&p   total payable:

Your name   (as it appears on your credit card or bank statement)

Your address including your postcode – should the order be delivered
to this address? Yes/ no

Your telephone number (including STD code)
Your email address
I do/ do not wish to hear about new publications from CTBI via email
Please make cheques payable to:CTBI Publications (MPH)
Your credit/ debit card details: Mastercard/ Visa/ Switch (delete as
appropriate)
Card number:

Card expiry date   Card start date   Issue number

Your signature   Date:

Delivery address (if different from above)

Prosperity with a Purpose: Exploring the Ethics of Affluence

ISBN Paperback 085169 309 1 price £11.99

Large print ISBN 0 85169 312 1
Hardback   ISBN 0 85169 313 X
Please see website - www.ctbi.org.uk/pwap - for details.

Essential reading for those who want to think intelligently about the pursuit of justice in the modern world, the authors of this collection of essays make a number of challenging policy proposals in areas where change is urgently needed. Some of the questions addressed here are:

How do we live a moral life amid such new wealth?
What are the paradoxes of prosperity?
How are the poor to achieve their just share of new prosperity in these islands and abroad?
How is this new prosperity harming the global environment?

This collection – *Exploring the Ethics of Affluence* - is produced to give substance to the shorter *Prosperity with a Purpose: Christians and the Ethics of Affluence* (ISBN 085169 310 5 price £3.99, produced by CTBI and the Executive Committee of Church and Society, written by Clifford Longley). The essays go deeper into new questions arising about poverty and prosperity in these islands and worldwide, and carry only the authority of the authors.

Order your copy direct from our website: www.ctbi.org.uk/pwap
NB Orders will be processed by and despatched from our distributor, CTBI Publications, 4 John Wesley Road, Werrington, Peterborough, PE4 6ZP

Have your say – join Clifford Longley and the team on the *Prosperity with a Purpose* Forum – www.ctbi.org.uk/pwap